SWU-MED-001

MEDIEVAL KNIGHTS 1100-1476

Giovanni Garuti
Nadir Durand

SOLDIERSHOP PUBLISHING

AUTHOR

Giovanni Garuti, Talented Italian artist. Illustrator that has worked with specialized Italian publishing: EMI, Albertelli, Soldiershop, Military Library. Many of his works are in private collections in Italy and abroad. Garuti is also a member of AMIS group of Milan and is an active member of the reenactor group *"Les Gardes Françoises"*.

Mario Nadir Durand, Italian illustrator, now retired bank accountant. He grows from childhood a passion for history and military costumes and uniforms and in general. Do not neglect any historical period, making for several years a few thousand tables of armed soldiers. He has already illustrated several Soldiershop books.

ACKNOWLEDGEMENTS

A Special Thanks to Mr. Ivo Fossati owner of EMI publications for his kindly permission to use some images of his works used in the book.

Title: **MEDIEVAL KNIGHTS 1100-1476**

By Giovanni Garuti e Nadir Durand. First paperback edition August 2016 by Soldiershop.
Cover & Art Design: Luca S. Cristini.
ISBN code: 978-88-93271134 - ISBN ebook code: 978-88-96519202
Published by Soldiershop publishing, via Padre Davide, 7 - 24050 Zanica (BG) ITALY. www.soldiershop.com

Publishing's notes

MEDIEVAL
KNIGHTS
1100-1476

Men at arms in battle XV Cent. From the "Combat des Trente (Le_Baud)"

PREFACE

This book devoted to the medieval uniforms uses the presence in the first part of the book of 17 marvelous tables realized by the Italian artist Giovanni Garuti. In the second part are several plates illustrated by the other Italian artist Mario Nadir Durand. Every table are equipped by a rich text that well describes the history of the character and illustrates his uniform. There are also present a lot of tables with adding heraldic shields of the various factions and noble families. The thematic of the subjects includes noble Italian families, Crusade order as the Hospitallers and the Teutonic. Noble French, German and English families. all in one historical period that has gone since 1100 to the late XV century. In Italian area are present and described some knights of Tuscany Lombardy : From Farinata degli Uberti, to the Tartaglia, to Jacopo de Pazzi just to the family Pellari and still Florentine militias and lombarde. In the crusade orders different Teutonic knights of Danish or German Area and a beautiful hospitaller knight. Among the German noble, English and French we remember: Wolfram Von Eschenbach (1170-1220), Ludwig IV of Bayern (1287- 1347), Aymer de Valence (1270-1324), Edmund Crouchback (1244-1296), Alphonse X the wise man (1221-1284) and Alphonse of Poitiers (1220-1271).

ITALIAN TEXT:

Questo libro dedicato alle divise medievali si avvale della presenza di 17 meravigliose tavole realizzate dall 'artista italiano Giovanni Garuti nella prima parte del libro. Di altre tavole realizzate da Mario Nadir Durnad nella seconda e conclusiva parte del libro. Ogni tavola e corredata da un ricco testo che ne descrive la storia del personaggio e illustra la sua uniforme. Sono anche presenti in molte tavole, scudi araldici delle varie fazioni e famiglie nobili. La tematica dei soggetti comprende nobili famiglie italiane, ordini crociati come gli Ospitalieri e i teutonici. Nobili famiglie francesi, tedesche ed inglesi. tutte in un periodo storico che va dal 1100 al tardo 400. In ambito italiano sono descritti soprattutto armati e cavalieri di area toscana e lombarda: Da Farinata degli Uberti , al Tartaglia, a Jacopo de Pazzi fino alla famiglia Pellari ed ancora milizie fiorentine e lombarde. Negli ordini crociati diversi cavalieri teutonici di area tedesco danese e un bel cavaliere ospitalliere. Fra i nobili tedeschi, inglesi e francesi ricordiamo: Wolfram Von Eschenbach (1170-1220), Ludovico IV di Baviera (1287-1347), Aymer de Valence (1270- 1324), Edmund Crouchback (1244-1296), Alfonso X il saggio (1221-1284) e Alfonso di Poitiers (1220- 1271).

Battle of Tannenberg 1410 (particular) from the famous painting of Matejko

MEDIEVAL KNIGKTS

BY

GIOVANNI GARUTI

AGNOLO DA LAVELLO NAMED *TARTAGLIA* 1370-1421

Agnolo Andrea's son was born in Lavello (Puglia) around 1370. It seems that he was nicknamed *"Tartaglia"* for a link stammer. Most of the news about his life come from biographies by other most famous *Condottieri*, such as Erasmo da Narni, Braccio da Montone and Muzio Attendolo Sforza. As a young man Tartaglia learned the military art serving in the Company Mercenary of Broglio di Trino, a minor Condottiero operating in centre Italy, it seems that Broglio took Agnolo under his wings and later he adopted him too: he died in 1400 and he gave Tartaglia by inheritance his name, his company and his personal banner.

In 1401 the company of Tartaglia strong of 100 lances was engaged by the Republic of Florence, together with Muzio Attendolo Sforza's company, strong of just 50 lances (one lance was formed by a variable number of mounted men, normally between three to five).

On 26 June 1-102 Gian Galeazzo Viscomi. Lord of Milan, advanced toward Bologna with his mercenary troops (including the one of Alberico da Barbiano). The Tartaglia's company should hold the Casaleccchio sul Reno's bridge. Barbiano with a clever encircling manoeuvre compelled Tartaglia to retreat and made a dash at Sforza s back. It was a total defeat. Tartaglia and Sforza were taken prisoners. Muzio Attendolo accused Agnolo of letting through the enemy.

This was a long enmity that was going to end in tragedy. G. Galeazzo Visconti could have conquered the whole Tuscany, but he suddenly died. Florence, feeling free from the threat of Visconti decided to siege and conquer Pisa: both Tartaglia and Sforza's companies took part on the siege and distinguished themselves by their military skill.

In 1406 at Vicopisano during the siege Tartaglia declared that Sforza had tried lo assassinate him with poison. Pisa capitulated in October 1406.

In 1407 Tartaglia was engaged by the Republic of Siena with a force of 150 lances and 100 foot soldiers. A new war strategy, that was defined as *"Tartaglians"*, based on the swiftness of movement and lighting raids, starred lo take shape. It became typical in Centre-Southern Italy. In 1408 started the quarrels about the Papal election and Agnolo received several offers by the King of Naples Ladislao of Durazzo and he decided to accept, even knowing that they would put him against Siena itself.

The crisis was settled in 1410 when Ladislao King of Naples made peace with Florence and Siena.

In October 1410 Tartaglia look the defence of Perugia against Braccio da Montone. In November near Borgo S. Pietro Agnolo defeated Da Montone and nearly took him prisoner. In 1411 Tartaglia occupied Radicofani and gave it back to the Republic of Siena. In 1413 Ladislao King of Naples siege Rome to discharge the illegitimate Pope John XXIII. Tartaglia took part at the capture of the town together with his eternal rival, the Sforza. Agnolo opened a breach on the Roman walls near S. Croce and invaded the town with his company. He was then in pursuit of John XXIII.

In 1414 the King of Naples died and a peace throaty was signed. Tartaglia got from the Holy Seat the custody of the town of Tuscania and consequently became its Lord and Rector.

Toward the end of 1415 Braccio da Montone asked Tartaglia help to take Perugia, that was still under the influence of Naples Kingdom. Together with Da Montone Tartaglia reconquered many fortresses and castles between Perugia. Narni and Terni. with a force of about 1500 horses. They attacked Paolo Orsini, who then came to an arrangement. On 2 July 1416 from Rimini arrived the Army of Carlo Malatesta. Braccio and Agnolo got ready for the battle that took place at S. Egidio alle Capanne, in which more than 8000 men were acting. Tartaglia and Braccio managed to get a great victory. Tartaglia himself captured Carlo Malatesta. Braccio da Montone became Lord of Perugia and Tartaglia increased his dominions at the expenses of the Sforza.

In 1417 Braccio da Montone joined a conspiracy whose target was the capture of Rome.

Tartaglia joined with an Army of 1000 horses and 2000 footmen, occupying Castel S. Angelo and dismissing Cardinal Isolani. who called for help the Sforza.

On 17 October Sforza set up an ambush to Tartaglia in Tuscania, but Agnolo however managed to escape. In 1419 Tartaglia and Sforza were together again at the service of new Pope Martin V against Braccio da Montone and Erasmo da Narni. Tartaglia reconquered Orvieto and was appointed Gonfaloniere of Santa Romana Chiesa. In 1421 Agnolo da Lavello was in Aversa by Martin V's orders. The Pope worried the increasing power of the *Condottiero* and wanted his head, making a conspiracy with Braccio da Montone and the Sforza. This last captured Tartaglia at Aversa while he was asleep and handed him to the Podestà.

Tartaglia was beheaded in December 1421.

In our illustration We represent Tartaglia at Tuscania in 1414 in full tournament outfit. We know that the Republic of Siena presented him with a golden helmet, valued at 600 gold Florins, with a crest of rampant lion of silver, chiselled by a Senese goldsmith, as a reward for his services.

The helmet's crimson cloth and the mantling with three silver and three gold roses is documented with certainly The Tartaglia 's personal heraldry is composed by three gold bands on a silver field, symbol of ancient nobility. On the personal majolica founded at Tuscania. his heraldry has a gold lion on a blue field over. We took inspiration from this for the tunic of the Condottiero.

The rose represented on the bridles and on the banner is a symbol founded frequently on the bas-reliefs at Tuscania. because he was devoted to S. Maria della Rosa patrone of Lavello. The white "knot", frequently founded at Tuscania. represent the personal banner of Broglio, his adoptive father.

The horse's crimson shabrak was presented by the Republic of Siena, too: we have represented on it the Senese lion and the personal heraldry of Tartaglia.

Agnolo da Lavello named "Tartaglia"
1370-1421

LUDWIG IV NAMED *"THE BAVARIAN"*
1287-1347

Ludwig of Wittelsbach, Duke of Bavaria, was born in Munich in 1287. When the German Emperor Henry VII died (1313). The problem of succession arose: the empire was then only a nominal political formation. Actually Germany was divided in several Principalities either laic or ecclesiastic, whose Sovereigns acted autonomously.

The German Sovereigns were called electors because it was their duty to elect the person who had the right to be called Emperor of the Sacred Roman Empire. In 1313 Ludwig defeated Frederic of Hapsburg, called "the beau" in the battle of Gammelsdorf so becoming the main candidate to be elected Emperor. Thanks to the help of Archbishop Peter of Magonza.

Ludwig of Bavaria was chosen by the electors as the Emperor with the name of Ludwig IV and crowned in Frankfurt 19 October 1314 (on 25 November followed the official Election in Aquisgrana, traditional seal of the ancient Carolingian Sovereigns).

The Hapsburg and their supporters declared war to Ludwig who could only count on the help of the powerful John of Bohemia. This war lasted no less than eight years.

In 1316 Ludwig fought the Hapsburg in the battle of Esslingen without any appreciable issue.

In 1317 the Bavarian temporarily lost the help of John of Bohemia and the Hapsburg took the advantage and invaded Bavaria.

In 1322 Ludwig defeated definitively the Hapsburg in the great battle of Muhldorf on Ihe Inn, capturing Frederic the beau himself and afterward he was merciful toward the defeated.

From 1323 arose the problem of the Papal confirmation to the Imperial power. Pope John XXII should legitimize Ludwig's election with his own personal Unction as per the Carolingian tradition.

Ludwig however totally supported the Ghibelline party in Italy and the Pope excommunicated him. The Visconti of Milan and the Della Scala of Verona gave their full support to the Emperor who on 22 may 1324 emitted the proclamation of Sachenhausen in which the Pope was accused of heresy. Ludwig though managed to get the help of the clergy, including the Franciscan Order.

In 1327 Ludwig went to Italy. In Trento he met all the Ghibelline Chiefs including the Visconti.

In 1328 arrived in Rome where the people elected him Emperor of the Romans with the ancient ritual of *Acclamatio* without the Papal approval. John XXII tried to rise the people against the Bavarian, but his political status was very feable and very few answered the call. Answering to that Ludwig elected an *"Antipope"* Nicolò V and managed to be *"Uncted"* Emperor by him (4 august 1328).

In 1330 the Emperor went back to Bavaria without having made order in the Italian politics, but still very strong, because John XXII was losing many followers. The Imperial victory seemed very near when suddenly the Pope died. The election of Benedict XII even more intransigent of his predecessor drove the whole situation to a stall. In 1337 Ludwig formed an alliance wild the King of England Edward III and helped him in the war against France.

In 1339 the Emperor did not take advantage of the favourable situation and did not attack France, except for a short raid against Cambrai. Without any positive issue, conducted by his son Ludwig of Brandeburg and Frederic of Meissen.

In 1341 The Emperor chose to make an alliance with France. From then on the Emperor did not take any interest in foreign politics and worked exclusively to enlarge the possessions of his House of Wittelsbach.

In 1341 he managed to obtain for his son the ownership of Tyrol. In 1346 Carl of Bohemia made an alliance with Pope Benedict XII against Ludwig who was accused of Heresy and abusive occupation of the Imperial Throne, not having received the Papal Unction. In 1347 Ludwig of Bavaria died during a hunt. Carl of Bohemia attacked and ravaged Bavaria following orders of the Pope. He was then in his turn elected Emperor with the name of Carl IV.

The sketch is taken from a bas-relief in Magonza's Cathedral. Ludwig wears a yellow cloak with the black Imperial eagle in the centre as per the classical Imperial heraldry (black eagle with spread wings on gold field). The symbol on the Emperor's chest is exactly reproduced from the one of the bas-relief. The two eagles respectively on the shield and on the banner have been enriched with various ornaments. Besides it is very possible that on the bas-relief the Imperial sym -bol was simplified.
The bull's horns on the helmet may be related to the House of Ludwig who was Lord of High Bavaria as well as Wittelsbach. Contemporary chroniclers report that in the battle of Muhldorf the knights of the Emperor were dressed like himself and that's why in the drawing the banner holder wears a cloak similar to the owe of his Lord and the same goes for the page who curries the tournament helmet.
The armour is typical of the period between 13th and 14th Century, a mixture of mail chain and plates. The sword's hill is exactly reproduces from the bas-relief.

Ludwig of Wittelsbach, Duke of
Bavaria
1287-1347

WOLFRAM VON ESCHEMBACH
1170-1220

We know only a little information about the life of this poetknight. He was born in Eschembach, Franconia, around 1170 in a family of ministeriales, that is, servants of a feudal German Lord who had reached the rank of nobles thanks to the military profession.

His family reached nobility, but was not wealthy and so Wolfram had to put himself at a service of a Lord. He was certainly good in the military profession, but he was even better in the poetic art, so much so that he was invited at the court of the Landgrave Hermann of Turingia, well known to have given his protection to many German poets of the time.

At the court of Turingia he practised both the art of poetry and the military profession, completing several missions on behalf of his protector. To him the Cavalry was a real mission, an engagement for life, a choice that binds a man for all his life.

All that is very appearant from his works, particularly from his masterpiece the Parzival, a free interpretation of the unfinished Perceval of Chretien de Troyes.

Other important works of Von Eschembach are the Willehalm, a poem on the wars between Christians and Sarracines, the Titurel (of which we have only few frag-ments) and several short pieces of Amor cortese, love poems that in Germany were called Minnelieder.

He died around 1220.

The picture representing Wolfram von Eschembach in full combat gear is taken from a famous miniature of the Manessian Code of XIII Century at the Library of Heidelberg's University.

Some of the knights represented on the Mannessian Code wear golden helmets.

It's possible that is peculiar to some type of German Cavalry. Anyhow we wanted to be as faithful as possible to the miniature and so we represent Von Eschembach with a golden helmet.

On the miniature the two axes, heraldic symbol of the Von Eschembach Family look black, but that is caused either by oxidization of the varnish or by scratches on the parchement.

In reality the Von Eschembach arms shows two white axes (argent) on a red gules field. That heraldic symbol is also repeated on the helmet, on the shield, on the banner and on the horse shabrak.

MANENTE DEGLI UBERTI NAMED *"FARINATA"*
(?-1264)

Manente degli Uberti, Jacopo's son, nicknamed Farinata, was the most important representative of a Florentine Family, whose earliest documentary attestations date back to the XII Century. He be came particularly famous by the citation made by Dante Alighieri in his poem, the Divina Commedia. Already since 1215 when in Florence the two factions Guelphs and Gibellines were born, the Uberti Family took side with the Emperor's supporters. In 1239 Farinata was put at the head of Gibellines faction and in 1248 played an important part in chasing the Guelphs from Florence gaining a temporary victory for his faction. In 1251 the Guelphs re-entered in the town and, after a furious internal struggle between the two parties, got upper hand and, in their turn, managed to drive out the Gibellines. Farinata himself was banished from Florence and put him-self at the head of the Gibellines exiles taking shelter in Siena, a town notoriously bound to the Imperial faction. With the help of King Manfredi. Farinata reorganized the Gibellines Party in Tuscany.

He then managed to get the attendance of the Florentine exi-les, under his command, at the battle of Montaperti, 4 Sep-tember 1260, by the Seneses side. The battle was decidedly won by the Gibellins who slaughte-red the Florentine Guelphs. it seems that Farinata himself took part to the pursuit and the slaughter of the Florentine Army, an episode that was for ever remembered and that drove the Florentines to hate the Uberti family. Anyhow in 1261 the Gibellines Party could go back to Florence. Farinata died in 1264. After his death the Gibellines Party collapsed after the defeat of King Manfredi at Benevento (1266) by Charles d'Anjou. In the same year the Gibellines were banished for ever from Florence. Farinata degli Uberti was posthumously tried and condemned for heresy and all his Family properties were confisca-ted or razed to the ground.

We represent Farinata degli Uberti at the battle of Montaperti, cheering for the victory over the Florentine Gibellines. The heraldry on his shield and on his horse's shabrak is Uberti's hosehold ones. The armour is typical of the XIII century: pentolar helmet, chainmail worn over the aketon (a quilted jacket that was supposed to deaden the sword's cuts), knees guards of pad-ded hide with a metal plate in front. He is equipped with a sword, a shield and a lance carrying a small pennant with Seneses colours (white over black).

On the background another Gibcllinc knight rejoices over the victory among the fallen Florentines.

JACOPO DEL NACCA DEI PAZZI
(? - 1260)

In the "Book of Montaperti" the only extant fragment of the Florentine army's order of battle, during the campaign against Ghibelline Siena in 1260, appears the name of Jacopo del Nacca dei Pazzi. enrolled in the registers of the gonfalonieri of the Pone San Piero district's knights.

Jacopo del Nacca dei Pazzi was a knight belonging to one of the most ancient families of XIII century Florence. Among his noble ancestors was the legendary Pazzino dei Pazzi. the man who, after coming back from the first Crusade (1096 - 1099), boasted he had been the first Christian warrior to climb Jerusalem's walls. Me brought back from the Holy Land some fragments of the Holy Sepulchre of Christ. In Florence this legend was the origin of the tradition of the *Sabato Santo*, the day when the holy fragments were used to give oil sparks to light the Easter candle, which was afterwards carried in procession into the Santa Reparata Duomo among hymns and great celebrations.

In that fateful day of the fourth of September 1260 Jacopo del Nacca dei Pazzi carried the Florentine chivalry's standard on the Montaperti hills, lined with the first rank of Guelph knights. According to a Florentine legend, during the battle a knight called Bocca di Ranieri di Rustico degli Abati lighting for the Guelph party, but secretly involved with the Ghibelline party, drew his sword and threw himself on Jacopo del Nacca dei Pazzi cutting off with a downward stroke the arm that carried the banner.

Bocca degli Abati tore up the banner spitting with disdain on the red fleur de lys on a silver field, while Jacopo del Nacca dei Pazzi. mortally wounded, fell off his horse. The astonishing gesture threw the ranks of the Florentine Guelphs into confusion, while the knights supporting the Ghibelline party ripped away the red crosses sewn on their clothes, and put on the Ghibelline while crosses and started lighting furiously against their own men of the opposite party.

The terrible melee that broke among the men of the Florentine chivalry disorganized the line of battle and helped the Senese knights reinforced by the German knights sent by King Manfredi the leader of the Ghibelline party-in Italy.

The Florentine army was charged without any residence causing, such as tells Dante Alighieri in his masterpiece (the Divina commedia), the terrible slaughter that turned the river Arbia red. with the blood of the Florentine Guelph.

The plate shows Jacopo del Nacca dei Pazzi at the battle of Montaperti with other Florentine Guelph knights, just before Bocca degli Abaiti's fateful gesture. The knight wears a XIII century typical armour: a chain mail hau-berk, a chapel defer, a characteristic infantry helmet, but widely used by the knights because light and practical, chain mail jam-bus, leather knee pieces, reinforced on the front by a round metal plaque. The weaponry consisted of a XIII century sword and a shield held by a leather baldric. The coat of arms of the Florentine Pazzi family was described as: *"silver with three couples of crescent moons contrasting azur up and gules down, the three couples made two and one."*

The azur crescent in a silver Held denoted in Florence the family's ancient origins in Fiesole (Tuscany's small town), while probably the red crescent. opposed to the azur, recalled Pazzino dei Pazzi's Crusade against the infidels. With the lime the ancient Pazzi's coal of arms changed because of a privilege of the duke of Berry, who allowed them to wear his own arms: azur crusilly or two addorsed dolphins or and red crested. In the background is visible a knight bearing the banner of Guelph Florence: the red gryphon in silver Held, armed with sword (the typical symbol of the Guelph party).

CITY MILITIAMEN (ITALY, XIII CENT)
ENLISTMENT AND MOBILIZATION)

In XIII Century every citizen of centre-northern Italy between 16 and 60 years old should answer to the call of arms when neces-sary. For lower and middle classes 16 year was the minimum age to he mature men able to wear arms. If a town was ill war or threatened from abroad, not only the town itself, but also the outskirts were mobilised. In the main squares of every Quarter the bells were rung to call the people, everyone had to come immediately The ones who did not present themselves and did not have a valid temporary exiled. The exemption from mobilization could be reached only with the payment of a certain amount of money, varying from town lo town. This money was used to recruit other soldiers or to buy arms. Once gathered in the square the men were organized in Companies under the command of a citizen, possibly expert in soldiering. This man became Capitano d'armi (in Milan Capitano del popolo already since XII century and Gonfaloniere at Florence and Pisa).

The entity and the number of Quarter's Companies was variable. The Italian towns, following their size, were divided in Quartiere (four sectors), Terzieri (three sectors) or Sestieri (sis sectors). A sizable Quarter could make up several Companies and also groups of specialists like the balestrieri (crossbowmen) or the palvesari (soldiers armed with pavises). The knights were gathered together with the fool soldiers, but they had different Commanders. Actually only the well off citizen could afford the maintenance of the horses. The foot soldiers usually owned their own weapons or made them up personally.

The Comune provided some parts of the defensive armament. such as helmets, shields etc. Each Quarter had a pool where were stored the weapons of every Company. In some City certain pans of the armament could even be rented. However the majority of the foot soldiers managed to arm themselves with anything they could get, such as knives, axes, cutlasses etc. The Companies were named after the Quarter which in turn took the name from the Gate or the name of the most important church. Some Companies remained in town during the outside raids of the other Companies. Each Quarter was granted some pastures to forage the animals of the expedition. The various zones of the Comitatus such as the areas outside the walls of the town. were bound lo provide the troops with food. carts, horses and pack animals.

The term Comune was in that period understood like "community", so the Comune's area could be much bigger than the area of the town itself, like in the case of the valleys. The Milanese infantrymen represent the Company of Porta Orientate (East Gate). On the banner the relative insigna: a sable lion on argent field. On the shields there was the Comune's insigna: a gules cross on argent field. The men are equipped with quilted jackets and iron helmets. The offensive armament was made of long or short swords, knives, lances, axe. The Companies wore only the heraldry of the Comune (to be reco-gnized by the enemy), whereas on the banners there was the Quarters's heraldy (to show the gathering point during the battle).

HERALDIC SHIELDS

Top, from left to right: 1) Milano. sestiere di Porta Comacina. 2) Milano. sestiere di Porta Orientale. 3) Milano. sestiere di Porta Romana. 4) Milano, heraldry of the Comune. 5) Milano. heraldry of the Visconti family. 6) Milano. sestiere di Porta Nova o Nuova. 7) Milano, sestiere di Porta Ticinese. 8) Milano. sestiere di Porta Verccllina. Left, from top lo bottom: 1) Tortona. 2) Pavia. 1) Voghera. 4) Bergamo. 5) Val Camonica. 6) Valtellina. 7) Valle Lomellina. K) Bellinzona (today in Switzerland). Right, from lop to bottom: I) Rosate. 2) Magenta. 3) Lonate. 4) Legnano. 5) Lodi. 6) Mandello Lario. 7) Locarno (today in Switzerland). 8) Busto Arsizio. Bottom, from left to right: 1)Brescia. 2) Gallarate. 3) Varese. 4) San Colombano. 5) Monza. 6) Vigevano. 7) Angera. 8) Saronno.

AYMER DE VALENCE (1270 - 1324)

Aymer de Valence, earl of Pembroke, son of William de Valence, was born around 1270. He was a cousin of king Edward I of England, who sent him on a mission to Flanders in 1297. In 1302 he took pan in the peace; negotiations between England and Philippe IV, King of France. As a reward for his services he was given a fief in Scotland near Selkirk and there he started building a castle for himself. In 1306 he was appointed Warden of the Scottish mar-ches and was personally involved in the war that pitted England against Robert the Bruce, who desired not only the throne, but also Scotland's independence. During that same year De Valence made a surprise attack on the Bruce near Methven Wood and took his wife prisoner. Later he also captured Nigel, the Bruce's brother, condemned him to death and had him executed as a rebel to the authority of the English Crown. On the 10 May 1307 the Bruce took his revenge on Aymer de Valence, defeating him near London Hill: De Valence barely escaped with the earl of Gloucester, shutting himself up in his castle at Ayr. He endured a long and difficult siege, which was raised only after the intervention of Edward I himself. Knowing his end was near, the King appointed Aymer de Valence as guardian to his son, Edward II. The King was worried about the politically ambitious Piers Gavestone, an intimate friend of the heir to the throne. Sure enough, immediately after Edward I's death, the new King lavished many favours on his friend, spurning the English Barons. When he sailed to Boulogne to many Isabelle, daughter of the King of France, he even went as far as to appoint Gavestone regent.

The Barons immediately tried to kill Gavestone and seize back control of the Kingdom. De Valence had been ordered by Edward fl to protect Gavestone at all costs. The earl remained loyal to the Crown and carried on his duty as best as he could, until the Earl of Warwick succeeded in capturing Gavestone and him had executed, De Valence was one of the few Barons who always remained on King's side.

In 1314 three Barons refused to serve the King in the new war waged against Scotland. In August of the same year the Scotsmen, led by Robert, the Bruce, roundly defeated the English army near Bannockburn and Scotland attained a momentary independence. De Valence took part in the battle with all his followers. Aymer de valence died suddenly in 1324 during a mission in France, at the court of King Charles IV. Aymer de Valence is represented here before one of the towers which guarded the coast of Scotland. He wears a typical late XIII century armour: the head is protected by a helmet, worn under a chain mail hauberk. This helmet serves two functions: to support the Great helm and to protect the knight when he is not wearing it. The chain mail is worn under a robe decorated by the heraldic colours of the knight. The knee-pieces are made of leather with a metal plaque on the front, but by this time they can also be made entirely of iron. The earls of Pembroke's arms comprise seven bands alternatively silver and azur. Along the rim of the shield are clearly visible ten small red birds (martlets), each painted with the head on the silver band. Bear in mind that the coat and the caparison may not always closely follow the arms. In this representation of Aymer de Valence we have loosely followed the image engraved on his funerary brass, still visible in Westminster Abbey today.

HERALDIC SHIELDS

We reproduced some heraldic shields of English knights in 1314: from the first to the fifth, they represent knight of Aymer de Valence's retinue. Top, from left to right: 1) John Comyn of Badenoch. 2) John Lovel of Tichmarch Northants. 3) William Lovel of Norfolk. 4) John of Hastings of Bergavenney. 5) Aymer de la Zouche of Devon. 6) Robert Botevilaine. 7) John Bluet of Hants and Wilts. 8) William Deincourt. Bottom, from left to right: 1) Walter of Hakelut. 2) John Clivedon. 3) Bartholomev Enfield. 4) Thomas Ferrers. 5) William Cosington. 6) John Eure. 7) Richard de Burgh, the Red Earl of Ulster.

EDMUND CROUCHBACK (1244- 1296)

Edmund Plantagenet named "Crouchback" the youngest son King Henry III and brother of Ok future King Edward I was born in London on 16 January 1244. In 1253 Henry III tried to obtain from the Pope the government of the Kingdom of Sicily for Edmund, who has only 9 years old. The Pope however demanded an exorbitant amount of money. Together with many other conditions. So the king had to renounce at this design not to alienate his English Barons. But the Barons rebelled all the same, headed by Simon the Monfort. Earl of Leicester, who in 1258 managed to have approved by the King the "Oxford Provisions"' a kind of Parliament made up by a council of Barons. In the meantime Edmund was in Paris with hit mother Eleonor, trying to organize an army of mercenaries lo help King Henry, but they had not sufficient money. Notwithstanding that in 1265 Simon the Montfort was defied and killed in the battle of Evesham, so Edmund managed to return to England. Henry III not having be able to get hold of the Kingdom of Sicily, granted lo Edmund three of the best Counties of the kingdom (Derby, Lancaster and Leicester) and other territories in Wales.

In 1268 Edmund and his brother Edward got "the Holy Cross" from the Papal Legate Ottobono and left for Palestine, where they look part to several fights near St. John of Acre.

The nickname of *"Crouchback"* was given to him in that period, but the reason is not known because it does not seem that he suffered from some physical faults. When the brothers came back to England Henry III was already dead and Edmund wore his allegiance to Edward who had became the King.

In 1271 Edmund married Blanche of Navarre et Champagne and due to that marriage he got the title of count of Lancaster and Champagne. In 1276 Crouchback fought against the rebels in Wales, a war that carried on until 1282 when the chief of the rebellion Roger Mortimer was captured. In 1291 Edmund was sent to France to negotiate with Philippe le Bel the problem of the Fiefs supposed under direct English rule, but he did not succeed and more than that, the French King declared that England could not have any more claim to Gascoine. In 1293 Crouchback and John of Lacy negotiated directly with the French Cardinals as peace messengers, but they did not get any result so much as that in the following year Edmund, the Earl of Lincoln and other 25 Barons sailed to France with an invasion army of 100 horsemen and 10.000 foot soldiers strong. On 14th May 1293 Edmund was appointed Army leader for the Aquitaine, but he suddenly died three week later. His body wax taken back 10 England and buried in Westminster Abbey.

The plate shows Edmund in 1271, escorted by his personal page. The Knight wears a typical armor of XIII century: hauberck and jambes of chain mail, great helm. His heraldry was as follows: three or leopards on gule field typical of the Plantagenets dynasty. Thanks to his marriage to Blanche de Navarre he could add to his personal arms an azure label to nine or lilies (three on each point I symbol of the Counts of Artois (Blanche was the daughter of Robert d'Artois). The page wears a white veste with a red cross sawn on. to show that he was as at the Crusades together with his Lord.

HERALDIC SHIELDS

We reproduced some heraldic shields of English knights in 1297-98. Top. from left to right: 1) Roger Bigod, Earl of Norfolk . 2) Robert de Vere, Earl of Oxford 3) Anthony Bek, Bishop of Durham. 4) Peter Chavant. 5) Thomas Berkeley. 6) Philip Darcy. 7)Roger Mortimer. 8) Robert Torry. Bottom, from left lo right: 1) Ralph of Monthermer. Earl of Gloucester. 2) John Bedham. 3) John Deyville 4) John Segrave. 5) Ralph Basset. 6) Peter Corbet. 7) William Latimer junior. 8) John Cantelupe.

TEUTONIC KNIGHT IN PALESTINE (XII CENT.)

The origins of the Order of St. Mary of the Teutonics are yet fully confirmed by the historians. During the siege of Jerusalem (1099), a merchant, probably from Bremen or Lubeck, took care of the German Crusader wounded in fight. It appears that the Patriarch of Jerusalem realising the need of a reception centre for the Pilgrims and Crusaders of German tongue, approved the institution of that small hospital. That hospice was then put under the protection of the Virgin Mary; unfortunately the sources are so vague that one cannot tell the truth from the legend.

A document of Pope Celestino II (9 December 1143) put that German hospital under the supervision of the Hospitallers of the Order of St. John of Jerusalem: the authenticity of such a decree is still debatable but it proves the existence of a Hospital of St. Mary of the Teutonics.

In 1189 some merchants, apparently coming from Lubeck and Bremen, attended the Crusaders of Acre's siege on their own merchant ships. In 1191 as the town was taken by Christians, King Guy of Lusignan.

Allowed the Germans to build a hospital: nobody knows actually for sure if there is a connection between this institution and the previous one. Between 1193 and 1198 there was a definite confirmation of the German Hospitallers and its separation from the Order of St. John.

In 1196 a Papal Bull from Celestino III confirmed the institution of the Hospital of St. Mary of the Teutonics. In 1197 Emperor Henry V gave to the new German Friars their first European possession in Palermo.

In 1198 King Guy of Lusignan gave his definitive confirmation to the Knightly-Monastic Order and assigned to it the guard and defence of the Rocca and the Barbacan of the King at St. John of Acre.

The first elected Great Master (Hochmeister) was Heinrich Wallpot von Passenheim and it was allowed to the Monksoldiers to follow the rule of St. Augustin and so to wear the white habit and the white cloak, bearing a simple black latin cross.

The Knights of St. Mary of the Teutonics were so at the same level of the other two great Orders, the Hospitallers of St. John and the Templars. In a very short time they managed to be their equal together on the military and economic field. The conical helmet is typical of the XII century, but still in use on the beginning of the following century, especially in warm countries, such as Palestine or Spain.

Also the other pans of the armament are typical of the dying century: hausberg with hood of chainmail worn over a quil-ted leather jacket (akelon) insulating and soft, capable to deaden the sword cuts.

The legs and feet are also protected by chainmail. Here is as a Teutonic Knight would look around 1198: he wears over the armour, a white cloak with the same cross sawn on the left shoulder, typical attire of the Teutonic Order.

The armament is made of an almond shaped shield, painted with the Order's heraldy, a long sword, an axe and a lance bearing a white guidon with the black cross.

TEUTONIC KNIGHT NORTHERN EUROPE (XIII CENT)

When in 1226 Conrad, Duke of Masovia got to know about the recent exploits of the Teutonic Order, he sent an Ambassador to the Court of Frederic II to ask for a military intervention of the Monk-Soldiers against the pagan population (Vetero-Prussians), who incessantly attacked his lands. The Duke offered as a reward the land of Kulm (Terra Culmensis) and the Emperor confirmed that with the *"Golden Bull of Rimini"*. This document bestowed to the Great Master and his Knights the sovereignty on all the lands that could be snatched from the pagans (March 1226).

The negotiations went on until 1228 because of the Crusade of Frederic II in Palestine.

The final agreement was sealed on 30 June 1230 and ratified by Pope Onorio III. As a bandmaster (a kind of governor) was chosen Hermann von Balk, who went to Prussia with about a thousand men and started to fortified the lands given by the Duke of Masovia. From that moment a great number of German peasants pushed on toward the new lands owned by the Order and so the constitution of a new state was born. In the nearby Livonia another religious-military Order had already been established under the orders of the Bishop of Riga: the so called Brothers of the Sword (Schweribruder).

In 1237 they were incorporated in the Teutonic Order with a decree of Pope Gregory IX.

Between 1236 and 1237 the Order had to face a serious problem: the Mongol invasion from the East. Many Knights had to leave Prussia to face the new threat and the Prussians people took the opportunity to rebel against the Order. The Teutonics lost many fortresses, holding only Thorn, Elbing, Reheden and Kulm. The rebellion was put down only in 1242. On 5 April 1242 the Prince of Novgorod, Alexandr Nevskij, defeated a Crusader Army of about 5.000 men near lake Peipus (on this Army only 800 Knights belonged to the Order). However this defeat did not have much relevance on the Teutonic states.

In 1245 Frederic II granted to the German Monk-Knights the possession of Livonia, Curlandia and Samogizia. New Bishoprics were born and the Teutonics carried on, also by force, the conversion of the population just subjugated. The acquisition of new territories brought the Order in contact with new populations and so with new enemies, but the Teutonic State was already a reality.

The dream of Hermann of Salza have come true just a few years after his death and it was going to last well over the XVI century.

The Knight wears a helmet typical of the German area. It is a "Great helm" of a rather more conical shape in use only from the second half of the XIII century. Normally the Knights belonging to a military-religious Order could not bear any heraldic symbol.

Anyhow where the Church of Rome's control was rather bland, the high rank Knights allowed themselves not to follow this rule. Many miniatures of German area show Knights wearing Winged helmets.

The Knight's armament consists of a great sword of German type and an axe. The black cross sawn on the horse caparison was not obligatory. The same cross is sawn on the Knight's veste, on his cloak and it's painted on the shield.

KNIGHT HOSPITALLER IN PALESTINE (XIII CENT.)

Since the end of the third Crusade in 1197, the Hospitallers of St. John of Jerusalem and the other two military Orders (Templars and Teutonics) started a campaign of military strengthening, calling more Knights all over Europe and enrolling a good number of mercenaries.

These, very often, were recruited in-loco even from warriors of muslim origin (called Turcopoles). Contrary to the common belief, in the Armies of Military Orders in Holy Land there was a good amount of non Christian soldiers. The data we have from different sources arc not very precise, but they can give us an idea of the increased military power of the Hospitallers between XII and XIII Century. It appears that in 1168 the Great Master of the Order of St. John. Gilbert d'Assailly, to be able to assemble an Army of 500 Knights and Sergeants (the Brothers Servientes were only temporarily at the service of the Order) and about 500 Turcopoles, managed to spend all the money of the Order.

This Army was promised to King Amalrico I of Jerusalem for the invasion of Egypt. Between 1217 and 1221 during the fifth Crusade the Order could count on a strength of 700 Knights and Sergeants and about 2000 infantrymen including a good number of Turcopoles.

In 1233 during the siege of Hamas, a small Syrian town, the Hospitallers could bring up a strength of 100 Knights, 300 mounted Sergeants and about 1500 infantrymen. That was, according to the chronicles of the period, just the strength of the Hospitaller's commendary of Antioch. The total strength of the Order all over Palestine must then have been pretty remarkable.

In the battle of La Forbie, in 1244. the Order lost about 300 Knights and only about 20 managed lo escape. In the same battle more than 200 Turcopoles, over 350, were killed. Naturally one must not think that in these battles the whole force was employed because in every Palestine Town under Christian domination there was a Garrison of Hospitallers, not to talk about the Fortresses belonging to the Order. The most famous, Krak des Chevaliers, was in 1271 defended by 200 Brothers (Knights and Sergeants) and about 1.400 infantrymen and Turcopoles.

When, after the fall of St. John of Acre, the Order left Holyland and transferred the Headquarters to Cyprus, its total strength was about of just 70 Knights, 10 Brothers Sergeants and few other faithful auxiliary Turcopoles.

The Hospitallers of St. John, since becoming a Military Order (XII Century), were usually fighting wearing their monastic veste (the *cappa clausa*) over the armour. It was black with a latin white cross on the chest. Being that veste rather uncomfortable in battle and so responsable of quite a number of losses, it was replaced by a surcoat (by a Papal Bull of 1248).

The surcoat should wear the same colors of the veste. From 1259 the Hospitaller's veste became red with a latin white cross, sawn on the chest. That provision regarded only the Knights whereas the Sergeants wore black until 1278. The change was not sudden and many Knights carried on wearing black veste with a white cross: it appears that in the beginning only the standard bearer wore the new colors. The typical "eight pointed" cross, the actual symbol of the Order (The actual Order of Malta), was introduced in the first quarter of XIII Century, but its diffusion was also gradual.

A different mailer stands for the Standard, which since 1182 was a white cross on a red field, symbol of an Hospitaller Order's.

ALPHONSE X NAMED "THE WISE" (1221-1284)

Alphonse X. King of Castil and Leon, was born in Toledo in 1221, son of Ferdinand III 'The Saint" and of the German Princess Beatrix of Swabia. He ascended the throne of Castil in 1252 inheriting from his father a Kingdom occupying two thirds of the Hiberic Peninsula, so that in fact it was the most powerful Kingdom in Spain. His military and political work did not match his father's. Actually, as soon as he reached the (hrone he had to meet several acts of rebellion from Castillan Nobility. Some *Caballeras* even took side openly with the moors of Grenada and with the Muslim Raiders from Morocco. Luckely Alphonse X managed to stop the invaders coming From Africa, so saving Seville, recapturing Murcia's region and make up a fleet for the control of Gibraltar's street. Already since 1256 he tried to reach the Imperial throne because of his direct parental tine with the Swabia House. With the help of the Holy See he managed to be elected Emperor of the Romans, but in the same time, Richard, Count of Cornwall was also elected. Alphonse did not like the idea of a transfer to Germany and wanted to rule directly from Castil, but that was the cause of the loss of many of his supporters. In 1275 he went to Italy to be elected Emperor in Rome, but Pope Gregory X, whom he met in France, convinced him to renounce the title. Alphonse's Imperial dream was by then dead, also because his two brothers, Henry and Philip, openly opposed him and their rebellion forced him to run back to Spain as soon as possible, Philip headed a Noblemen's Party opposed to the Crown, secretly helped by Alhponse's father in law, the King of Aragon Jamie I, whose aim was the weakening of Castil. Immediately after the death of Alphonse X in Sevil in 1284, a revolt broke out for the succession. The winner was his son Sancho IV. Alphonse X was neither an able politician nor a great warrior, but he his remembered for his important work of literate, which gained him the appellative of *"The wise"*. He devoted himself to history, philosophy, law and even astronomy. His Court admitted the greatest Literary men from Spain of every kind of race or nationality. His more important works are the Historia General and his masterpiece in verses, the Cantigas de Santa Maria, a poem, about a Knight Errant (identified with the Count Garcia Fernandez, X Cent.), helped in his heroic deeds by the Virgin Mary. In all the miniatures of XIII Century Alphonse X "The Wise" wear a veste with the typical heraldy of the Kings of Castil and Leon: quartered in I and IV with a golden Castle on gules field and in II and III with a purpure rampant Lion on argent field. In the plate the king of Castil wears a different heraldy, black waves on argent field.

The plate is taken from the miniatures of the XIII Century, in the first edition of the Cantigas de Santa Maria, commis-sioned to an unknown Spanish artist by the King himself. That work tells the story of a knight of the X Century, when the heraldic symbols were not yet well defined. The knight represented in the Cantigas wears armour and dress typical of the XIII Century. Probably the miniaturist painted the scenes thinking of the people and heraldy he used to see at Alphonse's Court. It is possible that the face is just the face of Alphonse X and that the painter did that to pay homage to the King as it was custom in the Middle age. Anyhow this heraldy is strictly belonging to the Royal House of Castil: we can see it on many items that reached us and are now conserved in Spain, such as vests, sword hilts of the XIII Century, often belonging to the Infante (the Throne Heir). On the right Alphonse's personal squire bears his Master 's insigna and on the left a knight bears the battle standard of the Kingdom Cavalry: The Virgin with the Child on a red field.

HERALDIC SHIELDS

From left to right: 1) Kingdom of Castil, 2) Kingdom of Leon, 3) Kingdom of Aragon, 4) County of Navarra, 5) Ferrante Ibanez de Valverde, 6) Teobaldo I of Navarra, 7) Moncada of Catalogna, 8) King Jamie I d'Aragon.

CITY MILITIA
(TUSCANY, XIII CENT.)

When a town of Centre-North Italy went In war. the entire population, cither resident between the walls or belonging to the *Comitatus* (the Comune's controlled territory), was mobilized. In town the bells were rung lo call ait the male citizen able to wear weapons, while some officials were sent by the Comune town to the villages belonging to the *Comitatus*, to mobilize the local peasants.

The peasant enrolment did not have strict rules like the ones of the towns. Generally the officer brought soldiers and the people were forced to join, but that happened only under strict necessity.

Most of the times the peasants were quite happy to be able m take pan to a battle.

Seldom they had a tactical role and were good only to make up number of create disturbance, arson or looting. Being those troops very undisciplined noted, badly armed and prone to tremendous loss of morale; the Comune's Captains did not like to have them under their Command. A peasant, on the other hand, was only to keen to participate to a fight. He could get rich looting and very seldom he risked his own life, because he could always manage to lake lo flight. If, on the contrary, he found the courage to fight and distinguish him-self, he could get a good situation on the Town's Militia and rise his social status. Actually the peasants could only manage to arm themselves with anything they could find at home: knives, agricultural tools, shields made of bottom barrels.

THE PALVESARII.

The Palvesarius belonged to a very special infantry unit that needed a particular training. ' A *Palvesarius's* distinctive feature was the Pavese. a wide and tall shield, oval or trapezoidal in shape, nude of wooden planks, sometimes covered with hide. This weapon gave a very good covering to the man.

Some Paveses were as tall as the soldier himself. Actually the shields were very heavy so it was necessary to be rather strong to be able to manoeuvre them in battle. The *Palvesarius* also had a long lance, useful to keep away the cavariy and the attacking infantry. The *Palvesarius* were front line soldiers.

With their Pavesi they create a long wall impervious to the enemy cavalry in the mean time covering the crossbow men during the long lime necessary to reload their weapons. In the XIII Century the usual war lactic was lo send forward the Palvesarii followed by the crossbowmen and the archers.

As soon as they reached the chosen position, they stopped, trusted the shields on to the ground, while the crossbowmen started to shoot on the enemy lines. On a retreat the Palvesarius duty was to protect the retracing men. Generally they moved in strict collaboration with the crossbowmen with whom they constantly trained. Being specialists their wages were higher, like the pay of archer or a crossbowman.

The Palvesarii could form Companies, but not every town district could make one up. In smaller towns Companies were formed picking up men from different districts. On the foreground we can see two XIII Century typical peasants. lined up beside the Florentine Infantry. They wear typical hoods of rough wool of rather dull colour, leather jackets and trousers also of wool.

Weaponry is very crude: kitchen knives, forks, cudgels (sometimes with nails to make them more dangerous) and barrels bottoms as shields. A cord was threaded through two holes and looped to enable transportation. Seldom the peasants wear Communal insigna.

To the right of the peasants we can see a line of Palvesarii of Florence's Comune. On their shields is painted the Comune's symbol: gules lily on argent field or of the People, gules cross on argent field. An infantryman bears the banner of Porta San Piero district (gules keys on argent field, while another Pulvesaria bears on the lance the pennant of San Pier Maggiore (gules keys on gold field). In X1I1 Century Florence had two Companies of Palvesarii: the Red Company, whose flag can be seen on the front line and the White Company, whose flag can be seen on the background.

HERALDIC SHIELDS

Top, from left to right: 1) Firenze, sestiere d' Oltrarno. 2) Firenze. sestiere di San Pier Scheraggio. 3) Firenze. sestiere di Borgo. 4) Firenze, heraldy of the Comune. 5) Firenze. heraidy of the People. 6) Firenze. sestiere di San Pancrazio. 7) Firenze. sestiere di Porta del Duomo. 8) Firenze, sestiere di Porta San Piero.
Bottom, from left lo right: 1) Siena, heraldry of the Comune. 2) Siena, terziere di Camollia. 3) Siena terziere di città 4) Siena, terziere di San Martino. 5) Comune di Lucca. 6) Comune di Volterra. 7) Comune di Pistoia. 8) Comune di Pisa.

Tuscanian palvesary and men at arms
XIII century

ALPHONSE DE POITIERS (1220-1271)

Alphonse Count of Poitiers, D'Auvergne and Later Count of Toulouse, thanks to his marriage to Jeanne heiress of Raimond of Toulouse, was born in 1220 son of the King of France Louis VIII named "*the Lion*" and of Bianca of Castilla Brother of Louis IX (the famous Saint Louis), was invested with the title of Count of Poitiers and Auvergne on 24 June 1241 near Saumur. This investiture gave rise to the rebellion of many Poitou's Barons, such as the Lusignan, the Parthenay, the Prahec and the Chabot. Hugues de Lusignan (Hugues X named "*the Brown*") driven by his wife Isabeau d'Angouleme openly refused to pay homage to the new Count. Isabeau who was the widow of the King of England John "Sans Terre", claimed the possession of Poitiers's County for her son the King of England Henry III. On Christmas day 1241 Hugues de Lusignan symbolically destroyed his home in Poitiers to emphasize his separation from the King of France's politics. Henry III had so the excuse lo declare war to the King of France Louis IX, who summoned all his feudatories with their Armies on 28 April 1242. On the 4th May 1242 Louis IX together with his brother Alphonse de Poitiers, leaded an Army of 4.000 Knights, 20.000 Sergeants, Equerries and Crossbow men, together with about thousand chamois. Henry III landed with his Army in France on 13 May 1242. On 21 June the French defeated the English in the battle of Taillenbourg en Charente. During the campaign Alphonse de Poitiers was wounded by a crossbow quarrel. After the defeat Hugues de Lusignan humbled himself submitting to Louis IX. In 1248 Alphonse de Poitiers, pushed by Pope Innocent IV who he met on Cluny set of for the Holy Land. He came back to France in 1250 with a message of Louis IX for the Pope. As the King was still engaged in Orient Alphonse ruled in France on his behalf presiding the Kingdom's Council. To start another Crusade in Holy Land Alphonse sailed from Cagliari with his troops, but unfortunately a terrible plague spreaded on the ships and the expedition ended in disaster. Alphonse de Poitiers died near Savona in Italy on 21 August 1271: the day after also his wife Jeanne de Toulouse died. Their bodies were then buried in Saint Denis Cathedral. Alphonse de Poitiers wasn't a great warrior but he was very crafty in politics and, mostly, a good administrator of his possessions, so much that the Poitiers's economy reached the top of efficiency. As well as King Louis IX Alphonse had another two brothers: Robert, Count of Artois and Charles, Count of Anjou, who later became King of Neaples and Sicily.

In the colour plate Alphonse dc Poitiers, followed by Pierre Count of Bretagne and Amaury Count of Montfort, is leaving the town of Toulose. With them ride the Equerries earring their standards. They all wear typical armours of the XIII Century. Notice the cylindrical helmet with fixed facial masque, widely used in Northern Europe and in France. It was well valued by his practicality and lightness, together with good protection. Alphonse heraldy represent a shield per Pale sinister or Lilies on azure field typical of the French Royal house of the Capetes. per Pale dexter or Castles on gules field, to show the parentage with Castile (his mother was Bianca of Castile). The banner is Toulouse's one: an or cross with 12 points on gules field. Pierre de Bretagne wears this heraldy: chequers or and azure red lined with an ermine quarter, the same on the shield and the banner. Amaury de Monfort wears an argent lion rampant on gules field an the shield and the caparison, while the banner shows an indented gules and argent.

HERALDIC SHIELDS

We reproduced some heraldic shields of French knights of VII and VIII Crusades. Top, from left lo right: 1) Robert I. Comte d' Artois. 2) Charles I, Comte d' Anjou. 3) Baudouin II de Courtenay. 4) Jean Clement de Met 5) Jcan II deNesle. 6) Gilles Le Brun de Bailleul. 7) Jean d'Ibelin. Comte de Jaffa. 8) Guillaume III de Beaumont. Bottom, from left to right: I) Robert I de Courtray. 2) Ferry Paste de Chaleranges. 3) Henry II. Comte de Bar. 4) Jean I de Beaumont. 5) Thibaud IV de Champagne. 6) Thibaud II Comte de Bar. 7) Barthelemy de Roye. 8) Archambaud VII de Bourbon.

KNIGHT OF PELLARI FAMILY
(SAN GIMINIANO, XIII CENT.)

On September 4th 1260 a huge Guelph army of about 3.000 horsemen and 30.000 infantrymen led by a considerable number of Florentines rovinously failed in front of the village of Montaperti with the Ghibelline army made up of only 1.200 horsemen and 1.900 infantrymen, led by about 800 Sieneses. In spite of the remarkable numeric inferiority, the Ghibelline army gained one of the most incredible victory of the Italian medieval history completely destroying the enemy army. The Guelphs suffered enormous losses, about 9.000 dead, more than 15.000 prisoners, the death of Rangoni, the Florentine Captain, and more than 60 banners captured.

An enormous disaster which however the Florentines did not manage to exploit to their advantage even if Ghibelline party took years to recover. On the plate we represent some Guelph knights of San Giminiano. The town of San Giminiano joined the Guelph party mostly to contrast the eternal enemy Siena, a town of Ghibelline tradition. On the foreground a knight of the Pellari family and behind a knight of the Useppi family followed by the standard bearer of the San Giminiano Comune.

In the Comune s of Northern-Central Italy people with enough money to own one or many horses should answer to the Gride (mobilisation order given by the Comune). In the Tuscan Comunes the Grida for the cavalry was called *Chavallata*. All the male citizens between 16 and 70 years of age had to answer and to be engaged. Sometimes the Comune took upon itself the expense for the horses or gave some small reimbursement to the people with lesser income. In Siena more or less all the members of the merchant class, the strength of the Comume's economy, joined the *Chavallata*. In 1302 Simone Tolomei was at the head of the expedition Corps of 25 Knights and some Equerries.

In 1312 the Sienese Azzo di Sarreano took some 50 knights and 200 Infantrymen to Rome to oppose the Emperor Henry VII. In 1317 the Sienese supplied more than 150 knights for an expedition against Colle Val D'Elsa. After 1350 owing to the final victory of the Guelph Party, all the Families of Ghibelline tradition, protagonists in the famous battle of Montaperti, became themselves Guelphs. To named few of those, the Salimbeni, the Cacciaguidi, the Buonaccorsi. the Sansedoni. the Saraceni. the Cacciaconti di Torquemada, the Tolomei. the Renaldini On the plate the knight of Pellari family wears the typical armour of the Montaperti period. A chainmail with some metal plates and metal leg protections, the first step toward the evolution of the medieval armour.

The knight wears an arabesqued vest to protect the armour from the weather. Many Knights liked to wear very rich vests also in battle only to show their social condition. One can see on frescos and miniatures of the 13th Century Knights with richly emboired vests whose fabric was certainly coming from the Orient. Surely a custom of the Islamic warriors met at the Crusades. The heraldry of the Pellari Family shows two or flowers on azure Held. The Usappi's a truncated shield with an or rampant lion on Argent field. The standard-bearer of San Giminiano wears the Comune's colours or and gules. Notable the San Giminiano Standard of an or truncate red with an Argent rampant griffon. For the joining to the Guelph Party the Duke Carlo d'Angio' guaranteed the Comune of San Giminiano the right of show on its shield a globe or lilies on azure field the symbol of the Angio family.

HERALDIC SHIELDS
Left, from top to bottom: 1) Piccolomini Family. 2) Tolomei Family. Right, from top to bottom: 1) Saracini Family. 2) Cittadini Family. Bottom, from left to right: 1) Forteguerri Family. 2) Cinughi Family. 3) Cacciaconti di Torquemada Family. 4) Renaldini Family. 5) Sansedoni Family, 6) Buonsignori Family. 7) Salimbeni Family. 8) Guastelloni Family.

DANISH BISHOP (NORTHERN CRUSADES. XIII C.)

At the end of XII century, there was a great migration of the Christian populations (Germans, Dane, Swedes) toward the region around the Baltic shores. In those regions lived peoples still bounded to ancient pagan cults, even if some of them were already under the Christian Order's influence of the neighbouring Russian Duchies, The migration from the West became more strong and better organized. Mercantile towns like Bremen. Hamburg, Lubeck became the sinning point of the German and Danes peasants. That increased their importance. Inevitable was then the clash with the pagan populations who saw their own existence threated. The Christian conquered and imposed their religion by force. True Crusades were organized, not as important as the ones against Islam, but they made quite a progress to the Christianization and civilization of the Baltic Regions. One of the must famous promoter of the northern Crusade movement was Albert von Buxhoevden, Bishop of Riga, who also controlled the Order of the Schwertbruder (sword holders). Knights monk, who were later incorporated in the Teutonic Order. Being of an impulsive temperament, the Bishop did not mind wearing the armour and take part in the fight. To defend the borders of his Diocese he built many fortresses and organized several campaigns lo conquer Baltic regions. In 1219 Albert together with Waldemar the Great, King of Dane mark, planned a Crusade with the aim of conquering the Baltic shores. The Danes subdued many coastal territory and founded Tallin fortress. All that caused two reactions: the Roman Church started to show an interest in the northern Crusades, while obviously, the Russian Princes reacted lo the invasion of their territories. In 1224 was conquered Tartu, a town on the shores of lake Peipus and the whole Russian garrison was slaughtered. Tartu was later donated to his brother Hermann, who made it his Bishopric. In 1226 also the Order of St. Mary of the Teutonics moved lo Oriental Prussia and started an active collaboration with the Crusaders of north Europe. From 1234 the Order joined the Bishop Hermann von Buxhoevden of Tartu. In 1238 the Schwertbruder were defeated by the Russian in the battle of river Saule. to become then incorporated in the same Teutonic Order, On 5th April 1242 a Crusader Army of Dane, Swedes and Teutonic Knights under Hermann Bishop of Tartu himself was destroyed on the shores of Lake Peipus by the Duke of Novgorod. Alekxandr Nevskij. The battle became then famous under the name of the "*Battle of the frozen lake*". Tartu was then taken by the Russians. From that moment the Teutonic Knights were the ones who bowed the weight of the Crusades, until XV Century. A Teutonic Knight protects in battle a Bishop of northern Europe. In the XIII Century, especially in the German area, there were many warrior Bishops. Several paintings of the time show Bishops wearing armours with typical Great helm surmounted by a mitre (for ex. *Vita Karoli Magna*).

We here represent a Danish Bishop taken from a triptic of XIII Century, now in the Monastery of Logum. Denmark. On the shields a typical Danish while cross in gules field, hooked at the lower arm. The Bishop wears a chain mail over the typical leather vest. The red vest over the armour wears several small iron plates sawn on the fabric, typical of the German area. Also the Saint depicted on the triptic is represented wearing a similar armour. Since the Gospels forbid the use of the sword, our Bishop prefers the use of a more "merciful" mace. The Teutonic Knight who protects the Bishop with his shield wears the Order's colours. Both wear leader knee protections with iron plate. The banner in the background is taken from the triptic and carries the same while cross in a gules field, hooked at the tower arm.

HERALDIC SHIELDS
Top, from left lo right: 1) Shield of Patriarca of Aquileia (XII cent..). 2) Shield of Bishop of Arezzo, Guglielmino degli Ubertini (XIII Cent.). 3) Shield of Guillaume, Bishop of Parthenay (XIII Cent.) 4) Shield of Bishop of Arezzo, GuidoTarlati (XIV Cent) 5) Shield of Bishop of Feltre (XIII Cent) 6) Shield of Bishop of Durham (XIII Cent.).

MILANESE CAPTAIN D'ARME 1475

Novara fell under the tyranny of Francesco della Torre in 1272. The construction of the castle was initiated shortly after that date for initiative of the same Della Torre.

To that epoch the fortification was compound from a great central tower surrounded by defensive boundaries, that they also contained the building of the noble family novarese of the Tettoni. The castle was widened by Galeazzo II Viscounts, around 1359, thanks to the demolition of the Temple of St. Luca belonging wings' Order Franciscan and thanks to the dejection of the suburbs of St. Gaudenzio and of Sant' Agabio.

In 1475 the duke of Milan Gian Galeazzo Sforza strengthened the defences of the castle using the stones of an already existing small fortress, called "her citadel", situated out of the boundaries of Novara.

The ultimate transformation of the castle happened in 1557 for initiative of the Spanish governor of the city: the ancient central body of the fortification built by Francesco della Torre was demolished and her defended outdoor were strengthened and modernize to withstand to possible draughts of artillery.

DESCRIPTION OF THE MILANESE CAPTAIN D'ARME 1475

We have represented here a captain of arms to the service of the duke of Milan Gian Galeazzo Sforza. He wears a typical fifteenth-century armor; The helmet is a "salletto" typical Germanic, but broadly used by the infantries of the XV century in Europe. The armor is typical of this epoch of gateway among the second halves the 400 and F of the begin of the 500: a hood of iron sweater to rings, an"usbergo" also made by iron rings, on which spallacci, gomitiere and protection gloves of the hands and the arms are worn. Leggings, knee-guards and schinieri protect the inferior limbs of our warrior.

Its affiliation to duke of Milan is symbolized by the heraldry of Gian Galeazzo Sforza, painted on it "rondella", the typical round shield typeset by wood tables covered of leather, very used by the Lombard infantries in the XV century.

Its offensive weapons are a sword and a hammer d' arme.

The tunic that covers its armor (cotta d' arme) brings to the left the heraldry of the comune of Novara, symbol of a temporary service for the defence of the city.

THE HERALDRIES

1) comune of Novara 2) personal heraldry of the duke of Milan Gian Galeazzo Sforza 3) family Tornielli 4) family Caccia 5) family Cavalazzi (probable) 6) family Avogadro 7) family Nibbia 8) family Tettoni 9) family Da Castello 10) family Dalla Porta.

ENRICO V° PLANTAGENETO
AD AZINCOURT
-1415-

Durand 87

Henry V the great English king winner at Azincourt. Plates by Nadir Durand

MEDIEVAL KNIGKTS

BY

MARIO NADIR DURAND

CAVALIERE
TEUTONICO
1200 D.C.
Durand

Teutonic knight XIII century

CAVALIERE
MILIZIA COMUNALE
1200 De

Italian militia knight XIII century

FANTE
MILIZIA COMUNALE
1200 DC
Duramel

Communal militia, light infantryman XIII century

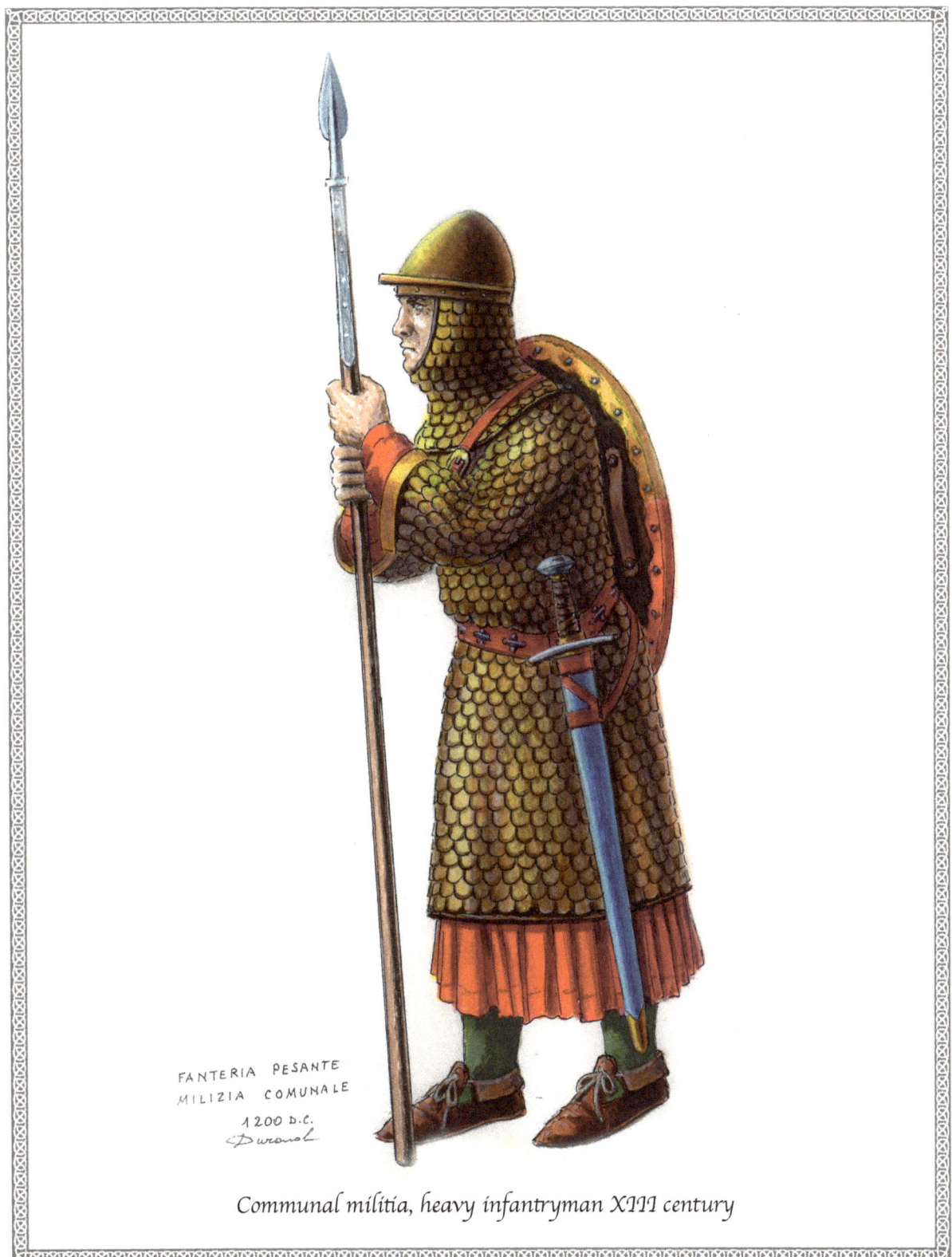

FANTERIA PESANTE
MILIZIA COMUNALE
1200 D.C.
Duranol

Communal militia, heavy infantryman XIII century

FANTE
MILIZIA COMUNALE
1200 D.C.
Durand

Communal militia, infantryman XIII century

SERRA GENTE
MILIZIA COMUNALE
1200 DC.
Durand

Communal militia, sergeant infantryman XIII century

FANTERIA PESANTE
MILIZIA COMUNALE
1200 DC
Durand

Communal militia, heavy infantryman XIII century

COMPAGNIA DELLA MORTE
MILIZIA COMUNALE
1200 D.C

Communal militia, death's company 1176

FANTE CROCIATO
1200 D.C.

Crusade infantryman XIII century

FANTERIA PESANTE
FRANCESE

French heavy infantryman XIV century

CAVALIERE INGLESE
1250
Durand

German knight 1350

JOHN DE WARENNE
CONTE DEL SURREY
1290
Duranol

John de Varenne count of Surrey 1290

CAVALIERE FRANCESE
SEC. XIV°

German knight 1400-1410

CAVALIERE FRANCESE
SEC. XIV°
Durand

French knight end of XIV century

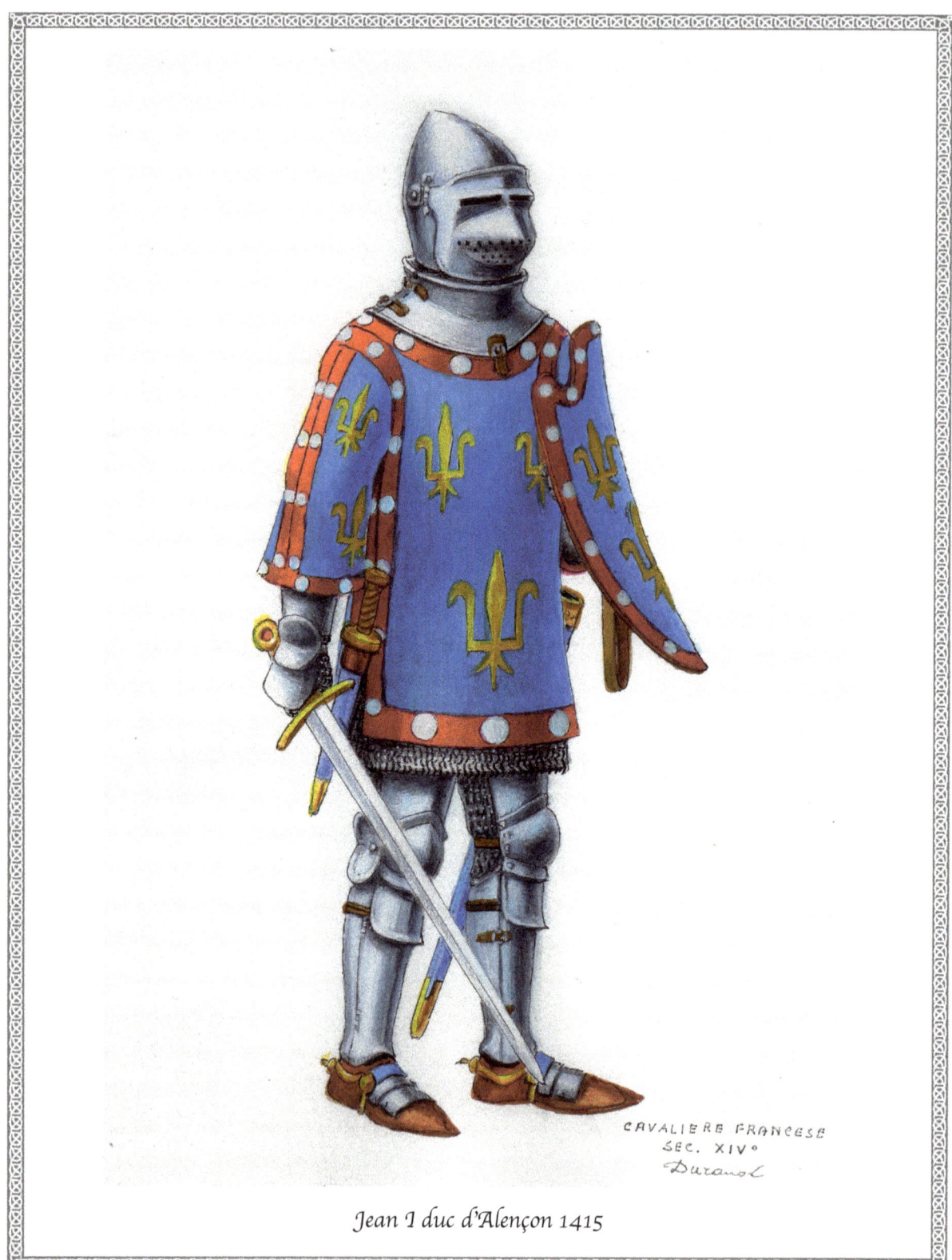

CAVALIERE FRANCESE
SEC. XIV°
Duranol

Jean I duc d'Alençon 1415

Sir John de Creke 1325

SIR GUY DE BRYAN
INGLESE
1300

Sir Guy de Bryan English knight XIV century

FANTE INGLESE
1300 D.C.
Duranol

English infantryman XIV century

PRINCIPE JOHN DI ELTHAM
1336
Duranol

Sir John Eltham 1336

CAVALIERE FRANCESE
1350

French knight 1350

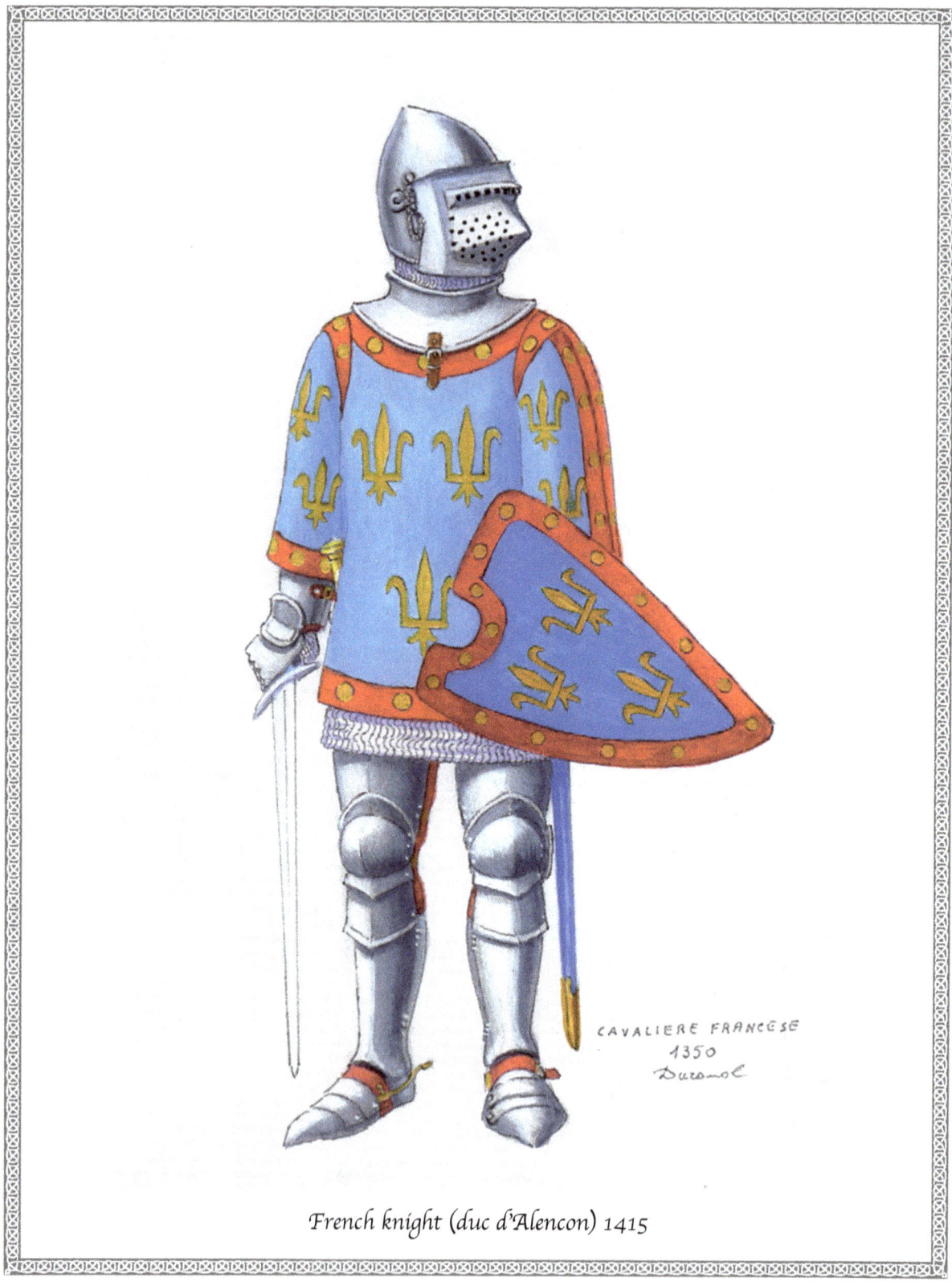

CAVALIERE FRANCESE
1350
Duramol

French knight (duc d'Alencon) 1415

BALESTRIERE GENOVESE
1350

Genoese (Italian) crossbowman 1350

CAVALIERE FRANCESE
1350
Durand

French knight 1415

CAVALIERE INGLESE
1350

English knight 1410-1420

SCUDIERO
DI
SIR HUGH CALVELEY
1351

Esquire of Sir Hugh Calveley 1370

Sir Hugh Calveley 1370

EDWARD
THE BLACK PRINCE
1375

Edward the black Prince 1375

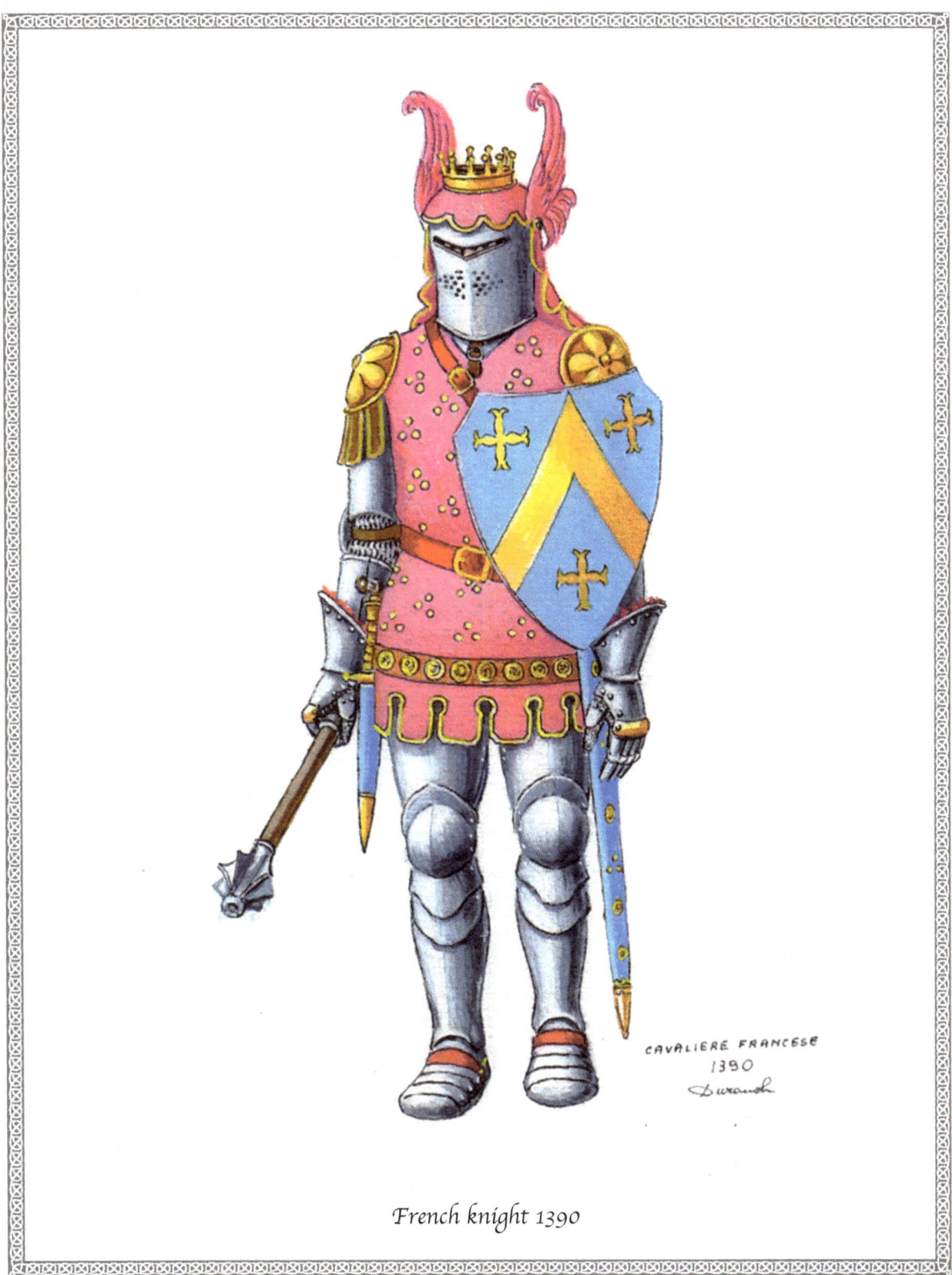

CAVALIERE FRANCESE
1390
Durando

French knight 1390

CAVALIERE FRANCESE
INIZIO SEC. XV°
Duronal

French knight 1350

CAVALIERE FRANCESE
SEC. XV°
Durval

French knight 1390-1400

BALESTRIERE FRANCESE
1400
Durand

French crossbowman 1400

ENRICO V° D'INGHILTERRA
AD AZINCOURT 1415
Dwianol

English knight 1415

CHATAR CRUSADE 1209-1229

The crusaders – The baron and its followers

(1) The baron in chainmail armour with bard horse. It's visible the internal part of the glove, made in leather.

(2) Assistant with hunting horn.

(3) Standard-bearer wearing a long vest on the hauberk.

The Albigensian Crusade or Cathar Crusade (1209–1229) was a 20-year military campaign initiated by Pope Innocent III to eliminate Catharism in Languedoc, in the south of France. The Crusade was prosecuted primarily by the French crown and promptly took on a political flavour, resulting in not only a significant reduction in the number of practising Cathars, but also a realignment of the County of Toulouse, bringing it into the sphere of the French crown and diminishing the distinct regional culture and high level of influence of the Counts of Barcelona.

The medieval Christian sect of the Cathars, against whom the crusade was directed, originated from a reform movement within the Bogomil churches of Dalmatia and Bulgaria calling for a return to the Christian message of perfection, poverty and preaching. The reforms were a reaction against the often scandalous and dissolute lifestyles of the Catholic clergy in southern France. Their theology was basically dualist. Several of their practices, especially their belief in the inherent evil of the physical world, which conflicted with the doctrines of the Incarnation of Christ and transubstantiation, brought them the ire of the Catholic establishment. They became known as the Albigensians, because there were many adherents in the city of Albi and the surrounding area in the 12th and 13th centuries.

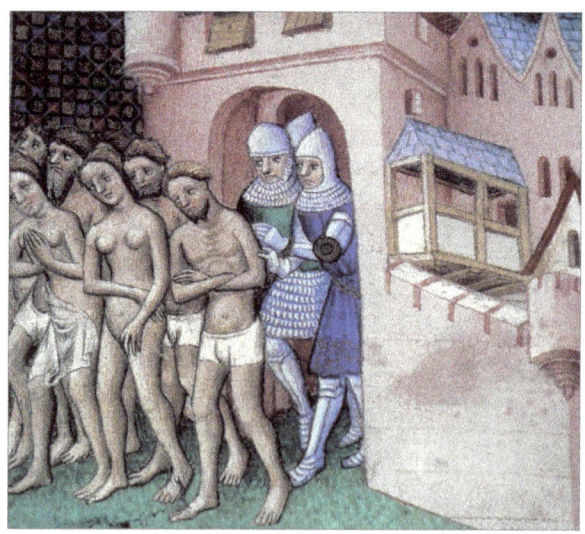

CHATAR CRUSADE 1209-1229

The crusaders - Enforcements from Other-European countries

(1) Miles of the Duke of Lorraine familia (probably fighting for the Duke of Burgundy) wearing a chainmail armour. The ruff is directly hooked at the masked helm.

(2) Servente of the Brienne family wearing chainmail armour with leather parts for arms and shoulder, leather gloves and leather ruff. The red-colored chapeau -de-fer probably indicates the soldier as a low-level rank.

(3) Contractor miles from Lombardy with notably cage-helmet.

CHATAR CRUSADE 1209-1229

The death of Simon de Montfort at the Siege of Toulouse (1218)
Simon IV of Montfort, lord of Montfort-l'Amaury, 5th earl of Leicester (c.1175 – 25 June 1218), also known as Simon de Montfort the elder, was a French warlord who took part in the Fourth Crusade (1202–1204) and was a prominent leader of the Albigensian Crusade. He died at the siege of Toulouse in 1218.

Last year..
..Simon de Monfort was an energetic campaigner, rapidly moving his forces to strike at those who had broken their faith with him - and there were many, as local lords switched sides whenever the moment seemed propitious. The Midi was a warren of small fortified places, as well as home to some highly fortified cities, such as Toulouse, Carcassonne and Narbonne. Simon showed ruthlessness and daring as well as being particularly brutal with those who betrayed their pledges - as for example, Martin Algai, lord of Biron. In 1213 Simon defeated Peter II of Aragon at the Battle of Muret. This completed the defeat of the Albigensians, but Simon carried on the campaign as a war of conquest. He was appointed lord over all the newly acquired territory as Count of Toulouse and Duke of Narbonne (1215). He spent two years in warfare in many parts of Raymond's former territories; he besieged Beaucaire, which had been taken by Raymond VII of Toulouse, from 6 June 1216 to 24 August 1216.
Raymond spent most of this period in the Crown of Aragon, but corresponded with sympathisers in Toulouse. There were rumours in September 1216 that he was on his way to Toulouse. Abandoning the siege of Beaucaire, Simon partially sacked Toulouse, perhaps intended as punishment of the citizens. Raymond returned in October 1217 to take possession of Toulouse. Simon hastened to besiege the city, meanwhile sending his wife, Alix de Montmorency, with bishop Foulques of Toulouse and others, to the French court to plead for support. After maintaining the siege for nine months, Simon was justly killed on 25 June 1218 while combating a sally by the besieged. His head was smashed by a stone from a mangonel, operated, according to one source, by the *donas e tozas e mulhers* ("ladies, girls and women") of Toulouse.
He was buried in the Cathedral of Saint-Nazaire at Carcassonne. His body was later moved by one of his sons to be reinterred at Montfort l'Amaury. A tombstone in the South Transept of the Cathedral is inscribed "of Simon de Montfort".

TUSCANY KNIGHT 1432

The Battle of San Romano is a set of three paintings by the great Florentine painter Paolo Uccello depicting events that took place at the Battle of San Romano between Florentine and Sienese forces in 1432. They are significant as revealing the development of linear perspective in early Italian Renaissance painting, and are unusual as a major secular commission. The paintings are in egg tempera on 3 wooden panels, each over 3 metres long. They are now divided between three collections, the National Gallery, the Galleria degli Uffizi, Florence, and the Musée du Louvre, Paris..

The knight of the battle

The knight on the left (1) are from the Louvre panel, a man at the order of Micheletto Attendolo, bringing the standard of this captain.
The knight at horse (2) are from the London painting, a man of Niccolò da Tolentino, the captain leading the Florentine cavalry. He had a reputation for recklessness, and doesn't even wear a helmet.

SOLDIERS, WEAPONS & UNIFORMS ALREADY PUBLISHED

At now in the paper books serie of **Soldiers, weapons & Uniforms** we have printed the first part of Viskovatov's work dedicated to the uniforms and weapons belonging to the Russian army during the Napoleonic period, until 1825. And a book on Austrian army from XVII century to XIX century.

Our new edition, the first ever published in English, both on paper and digital format, boasts a large number of color plates, many of them unpublished and colored by our team of expert artists of uniformology. Each volume is based on several color plates, always accompanied by the original translated text which describes the uniforms, the organization and the armament of the subjects.

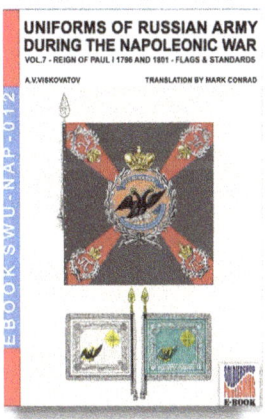

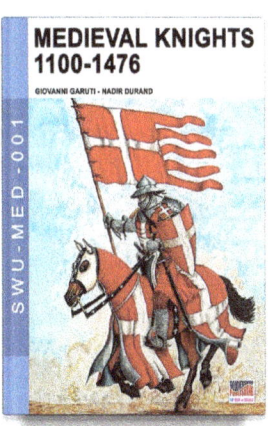

www.ingramcontent.com/pod-product-compliance
Lightning Source LLC
Chambersburg PA
CBHW041149120626
46547CB00020B/3162